MADISON IN FOCUS

A CITY'S STORY TOLD THROUGH PHOTOGRAPHY

presented by

ACKNOWLEDGMENTS

The Wisconsin State Journal is pleased to present "Madison in Focus: A City's Story Told Through Photography." It must be noted, however, that this unique pictorial history book would not have been possible without the generous contributions made by many people from virtually every corner of our community. We are indebted, first of all, to those early area residents who captured their time — our history — in photographs, and provided a glimpse into their lives.

Secondly, all area residents are indebted to the many individuals who are committed to preserving our history in various libraries, historical societies, archives and personal collections throughout our community.

The following organization has contributed greatly to this project:
Wisconsin Historical Society

FOREWORD

Flying high above the rolling Wisconsin landscape, sky-blue lakes, orderly rows of corn and tree-lined streets, observers find a picture-perfect view of Madison.

And as the decades march on, the trees below grow taller, neighborhoods expand and our sense of place strengthens. Left behind are compelling images of a beautiful community and its place in the world.

In these photographs, we see our collective determination, optimism, curiosity, spirit for discovery and pursuit of happiness.

We see the faces, places and traces of time.

We see joy. We see conflict. We see resolution. We see progress. We see ourselves. It all comes into focus.

While there are many books available about Madison, we believe there's no better showing of the face of our hometown than "Madison In Focus." Like the cover image of the early passenger plane high above our state's Capitol, we also believe it represents a perspective like no other.

Each chapter tells a story. Each image becomes a window into a way of life, a family, a business and a community of hopeful people. Each image transports us back in time, if only for a moment.

We hope you agree this book is as much an experience as it is a gift.

It's with great delight that we share it with you. We hope it will inspire you to share your memories of Madison with your family, friends and newcomers.

This book is the result of reviewing and selecting photos from hundreds of images gathered from Madison residents, the archives of the Wisconsin Historical Society and the pages of the Wisconsin State Journal. We offer our heartfelt gratitude to all involved in assembling such a memorable collection, including our partners at the state Historical Society and Smart Motors.

And most of all, we thank you for welcoming this book into your home. Each image was displayed with your pleasure and interest in mind.

The Wisconsin State Journal has been a guest in Madison area homes since 1839, and this book is our thank you for allowing us to tell the story of Madison then, now and well into tomorrow.

John M. Humenik
President and Publisher
Wisconsin State Journal

John Smalley
Editor
Wisconsin State Journal

TABLE OF CONTENTS

CHAPTER ONE
THE LATE 1800s

Even in the late 1800s, one could discover many clear hints of the things that would eventually give shape and form and definition to modern-day Madison.

The lakes, and their interplay with the city. Bicycles everywhere. Yes, even in 1897 the Madison cycling club made news when a few dozen folks and their bikes came together for a club photo. The university and its curious minds, too, were here from the beginning.

The first Capitol building in Madison in 1837 replaced the temporary one in Belmont after legislators decided on Madison as Wisconsin's capital city in 1836. By the late 1860s, construction was completed on Madison's second Capitol, as state government had outgrown the original building.

A fire in 1904 destroyed a large part of the second Madison Capitol, and the building was largely demolished and replaced one wing at a time. Construction on Madison's third Capitol, the much larger more beautiful version we know today, was started in 1906 and completed in 1917.

The years just before and after the Civil War were difficult for Madison. After peaking in population at nearly 11,000 in 1857, a sharp drop in real estate values and other recession-based fears caused an exodus of nearly 40 percent of the city's population.

Then came an expansion of the "iron horse," and Madison's receptivity to new railroad lines sparked great new productivity in the capital city in the late 1860s. Madison's geography – placed halfway between Milwaukee and Prairie du Chien, as well as falling conveniently on the rail pathway from Chicago to Minneapolis – helped the boom thrive and grow.

By 1875, Madison's population would again rise above 10,000. The city was thriving, and family names like Doty, Atwood, Fairchild and Mills were firmly in place. The university expanded, and the city's police and fire departments came into their own.

Madison was ready for the new century ahead.

OPPOSITE: The Railway Hotel at 641 West Washington Avenue, the Chicago, Milwaukee, and St. Paul Railway ticket office and passenger station, circa 1890s. COURTESY WISCONSIN HISTORICAL SOCIETY, IMAGE ID 11035

ABOVE: Panoramic view of Madison and the second State Capitol, top center, looking from Main Hall at University of Wisconsin with North and South Halls in the foreground, November 11, 1861. COURTESY WISCONSIN HISTORICAL SOCIETY, IMAGE ID 10495

RIGHT: The second State Capitol, circa 1861. The first Capitol building was a temporary structure in Belmont where legislators chose Madison as the state's permanent Capitol. The second capitol was erected in 1837 and used into the 1860s, when construction began on a new Capitol at the same location. COURTESY WISCONSIN HISTORICAL SOCIETY, IMAGE ID 3942

OPPOSITE BOTTOM LEFT: Hausmann's Capital Brewery employees on the corner of State and West Gorham streets, circa 1870s. Capital was one of five German-owned breweries in Madison at the time.
COURTESY WISCONSIN HISTORICAL SOCIETY, IMAGE ID 11692

OPPOSITE BOTTOM MIDDLE: The first floor rotunda of the third State Capitol, circa 1870.
COURTESY WISCONSIN HISTORICAL SOCIETY, IMAGE ID 23567

OPPOSITE BOTTOM RIGHT: View looking east up West Washington Avenue past the Northwestern Railroad depot, toward the Capitol, circa 1870s. A sign at the railroad tracks reads, "Look out for the cars."
COURTESY WISCONSIN HISTORICAL SOCIETY, IMAGE ID 11653

TOP: University of Wisconsin's Washburn Observatory, circa 1880.
COURTESY WISCONSIN HISTORICAL SOCIETY, IMAGE ID 26709

ABOVE: The rear of Bascom Hall (formerly Main Hall) on the University of Wisconsin campus, circa 1880.
COURTESY WISCONSIN HISTORICAL SOCIETY, IMAGE ID 57402

LEFT: Soldiers in formation at the corner of South Carroll and West Main streets during the United States centennial celebration, July 1876. COURTESY WISCONSIN HISTORICAL SOCIETY, IMAGE ID 11480

OPPOSITE: University of Wisconsin Class of 1876 at Main Hall (later Bascom Hall). COURTESY WISCONSIN HISTORICAL SOCIETY, IMAGE ID 27194

TOP: Wisconsin State Journal, office on East Washington Avenue, circa 1881. David Atwood, second from left with white beard, and a partner created the paper through the purchase of Madison Express. COURTESY WISCONSIN STATE JOURNAL

ABOVE: The newly built Science Hall on the University of Wisconsin campus, 1887. COURTESY WISCONSIN HISTORICAL SOCIETY, IMAGE ID 58992

RIGHT: Madison City Hall at the corner of West Mifflin Street and Wisconsin Avenue with the Wisconsin Avenue entrance to Capitol Park visible in the foreground, 1880. COURTESY WISCONSIN HISTORICAL SOCIETY, IMAGE ID 23534

ABOVE LEFT: Soldiers of the University Battalion march in a military parade down West Main Street to honor the visit of President Grover Cleveland, October 7, 1887.
COURTESY WISCONSIN STATE JOURNAL

ABOVE: A military parade progresses up King Street toward the Capitol in celebration of President Grover Cleveland's visit on October 8, 1887.
COURTESY WISCONSIN HISTORICAL SOCIETY, IMAGE ID 37376

LEFT: Bascom Hall, University of Wisconsin, circa 1890.
COURTESY WISCONSIN STATE JOURNAL

ABOVE: The dedication ceremony for the University of Wisconsin Armory and Gymnasium (also known as Old Red or Red Gym), circa 1894. COURTESY WISCONSIN HISTORICAL SOCIETY, IMAGE ID 67852

RIGHT: The pharmaceutical laboratory at the University of Wisconsin, circa 1890. COURTESY WISCONSIN HISTORICAL SOCIETY, IMAGE ID 39003

OPPOSITE: The water tower at the top of East Washington Avenue, circa 1890s. COURTESY WISCONSIN HISTORICAL SOCIETY, IMAGE ID 3507

ABOVE: A fire department ladder wagon speeding around the corner of South Pinckney and East Main streets, circa 1895.
COURTESY WISCONSIN HISTORICAL SOCIETY, IMAGE ID 23468

ABOVE RIGHT: The Hausmann Brewery Bar, circa 1895.
COURTESY WISCONSIN HISTORICAL SOCIETY, IMAGE ID 3054

RIGHT: Madison Police, circa 1890s. Front row, from left: Frank Currier, Chief John Adamson, Jake Togsland, John Scherer. Back row: Tom Shaughnessy, Jake Behrend, Arne K., Alex O'Neill. COURTESY WISCONSIN HISTORICAL SOCIETY, IMAGE ID 36081

ABOVE: The city ambulance (left) and police wagons at the Madison Police Department station, 14-16 South Webster Street, circa 1890s. COURTESY WISCONSIN HISTORICAL SOCIETY, IMAGE ID 67016

ABOVE LEFT: University of Wisconsin boathouse on Lake Mendota, circa 1895. The armory and gymnasium building (also known as Old Red or the Red Gym) is in the background. COURTESY WISCONSIN HISTORICAL SOCIETY, IMAGE ID 67885

LEFT: University of Wisconsin gymnasium, circa 1895. COURTESY WISCONSIN HISTORICAL SOCIETY, IMAGE ID 57626

ABOVE: Railroad employees with Chicago, Milwaukee, and St. Paul Locomotive #280 at the Madison Roundhouse, 1896. From left are firemen P.D. Connelly, James Schelgham, and Frank Buchanan; switchman "Duck" Murphy, firemen Omro B. Mills (on gangway) and Ed Schewenk; yard foreman Paul Dweites; and engineers Jack Fitzgerald and Theo Torgeson.
COURTESY WISCONSIN HISTORICAL SOCIETY, IMAGE ID 24818

LEFT: South Hall, Music Hall and Science Hall over Langdon Street, circa 1897.
COURTESY WISCONSIN HISTORICAL SOCIETY, IMAGE ID 67870

OPPOSITE: Cycling club, 1897. COURTESY WISCONSIN HISTORICAL SOCIETY, IMAGE ID 98615

ABOVE: The 15th wedding anniversary of Mr. and Mrs. Proudfit, December 8, 1898. Front row, from left: O.D. Brandenburg, Professor David B. Frankenburger, Elizabeth Proudfit, Mr. Proudfit, Mrs. Proudfit, Josephine Proudfit, A.B. Morris, Frank Proudfit. Second row: Harry Hobbins, Mrs. Hobbins, Mrs. David B. Frankenburger, Mrs. Frank Brown, Mrs. Levi M. Vilas, Mrs. O.D. Brandenburg, Mrs. Fred Brown, Mrs. Samuel H. Marshall, Mr. Marshall, Mrs. A.B. Morris. Back row: Miss Mary Louise Atwood, Mrs. Louis M. Hanks, Mr. Hanks, Fred M. Brown, Mrs. William S. Marshall, Professor Marshall, Frank Brown, Mrs. Stanley C. Hanks, Mr. Hanks, Mrs. Henry Vilas, Mr. Vilas, Mrs. Fred Spensley and Mr. Spensley, Mrs. Carl A. Johnson, Mr. Johnson, Mrs. Frank Edsall, Dr. Edsall, Frank Allis, Mrs. Frank Allis. COURTESY WISCONSIN HISTORICAL SOCIETY, IMAGE ID 41267

RIGHT: State Street from Bascom Hill, 1896.
COURTESY WISCONSIN HISTORICAL SOCIETY, IMAGE ID 1893

OPPOSITE TOP: University Heights and the University of Wisconsin football field, 1898. The football field was the site of Camp Randall during the Civil War. COURTESY WISCONSIN HISTORICAL SOCIETY, IMAGE ID 2225

OPPOSITE BOTTOM LEFT: City of Madison attorney Gilbert Row in his office on the second floor of the Fairchild Block at 29 East Main Street, circa 1898. COURTESY WISCONSIN HISTORICAL SOCIETY, IMAGE ID 30328

OPPOSITE BOTTOM RIGHT: The University of Wisconsin armory and gymnasium (also known as the Red Gym or Old Red) on Langdon Street, circa 1898. COURTESY WISCONSIN HISTORICAL SOCIETY, IMAGE ID 57047

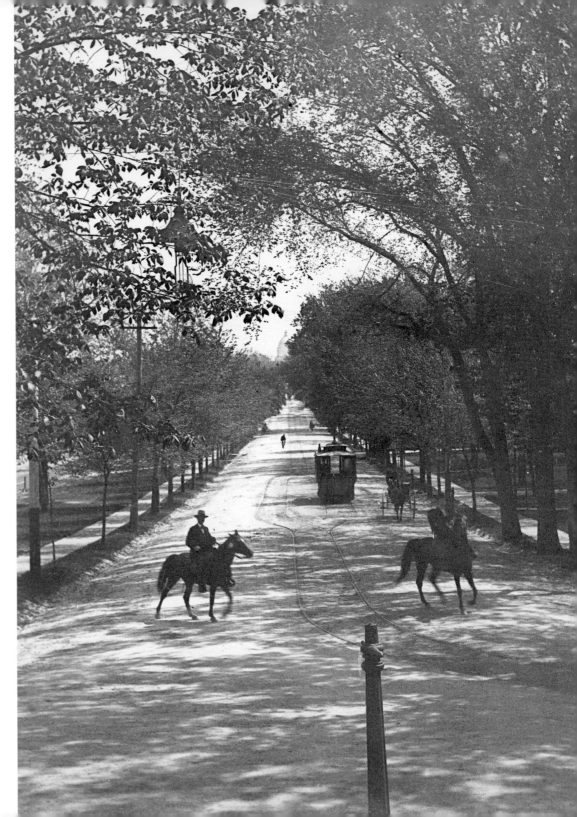

ABOVE: Chicago and Northwestern Railroad station at 219 South Blair Street at East Wilson Street, circa 1909. COURTESY WISCONSIN HISTORICAL SOCIETY, IMAGE ID 2258

OPPOSITE: The area of Madison behind Main Hall (later Bascom Hall) in 1899. COURTESY WISCONSIN STATE JOURNAL

CHAPTER TWO

THE EARLY 1900s

Like everywhere in the United States, a long-brewing theme in Madison in the early 1900s was war. The escalating military conflict in Europe was only a remote concern until May 7, 1915, when a German U-boat sank the British ocean liner Lusitania.

With 128 Americans among the dead, public opinion in the U.S. toward Germany changed suddenly, and two years later, on April 6, 1917, the Wisconsin State Journal would shout, "WAR IS DECLARED." A month later, the first Madison servicemen left for basic training in Fort Sheridan, Ill. Soon after, a national draft lottery was established, and the newspaper printed two "extra" editions to inform local residents of the names of Madison men called to duty.

Among the local volunteers was Col. Joseph W. (Bud) Jackson. A successful businessman and former cowboy, Jackson organized the Army's last mounted cavalry unit while serving under Gen. John J. "Black Jack" Pershing. Another well-known businessman from Madison who fought in the war was Oscar Rennebohm, who served two years in the Navy before coming home to launch his successful drugstore chain. Rennebohm later was elected Wisconsin governor in 1948.

Meanwhile, back on the home front, Madison continued to grow, and to change. Names like Bascom, La Follette and Van Hise were making their mark on the University of Wisconsin and beyond. John Bascom, elected president of the university in 1874, led UW from a purely teaching institution into an era of science and research in the early 1900s.

Two of Bascom's most famous students were Robert M. La Follette and Charles Van Hise. The former went on to a long and industrious political career in Wisconsin, while the latter would become university president in 1904. Van Hise coined the concept that a university should be a servant of the state to which it belongs – a premise that became known as the Wisconsin Idea.

OPPOSITE: World War I draftees at the Chicago and Northwestern Depot, 201 South Blair Street, on their way to basic training and then France, May 25, 1918. Nearly 3,000 Madison men joined the war effort. COURTESY WISCONSIN HISTORICAL SOCIETY, IMAGE ID 11039

ABOVE: Wisconsin State Journal staff at the office on East Washington Avenue, circa 1900. From left: Robert Slightam, printer; Walter Reimer, linotype operator; Herbert Schillinger, "printer's devil"; Alvin Shower, printer; Michael Wald, stereotyper; Gladys Fowler, proofreader; Frank Esser, makeup man; Mrs. Klusman-Wissler, proofreader; Charles Wald, book department foreman; Amos P. Wilder, editor and publisher; Grace Green, proofreader; Thomas S. Morris, business manager; Edward Wissler, business office; "Ned" Jordan, reporter; Red W. Arthur, proofreader; George S. Post, foreman of the press room; Carl Morris, business office; Theodore Wilson, linotype operator; Ben Parsons, foreman of the job department. COURTESY WISCONSIN STATE JOURNAL

ABOVE RIGHT: Matthew J. Hoven in front of his meat market at the corner of North Hamilton and East Mifflin streets, circa 1900. COURTESY WISCONSIN HISTORICAL SOCIETY, IMAGE ID 11037

RIGHT: University of Wisconsin freshman women's basketball team in the gymnasium at Ladies Hall (later Chadbourne Hall), circa 1900. COURTESY WISCONSIN HISTORICAL SOCIETY, IMAGE ID 2263

OPPOSITE: Horse and buggies parked along East Washington Avenue in front of the Wisconsin State Journal building, circa 1900. COURTESY WISCONSIN STATE JOURNAL

ABOVE: The W.H. Rogers Hook & Ladder Co. horse-drawn wagon in front of the Central Fire Station at 10 South Webster Street, circa 1902.
COURTESY WISCONSIN HISTORICAL SOCIETY, IMAGE ID 41758

ABOVE RIGHT: Steamboats docked on Lake Monona, circa 1900.
COURTESY WISCONSIN HISTORICAL SOCIETY, IMAGE ID 47494

RIGHT: An iceboat owned by Dutton and Wheeler on Lake Mendota, circa early 1900s.
COURTESY WISCONSIN HISTORICAL SOCIETY, IMAGE ID 60498

ABOVE: Madison Fire Department hose wagon near the intersection of Webster Street and East Washington Avenue, circa 1902. COURTESY WISCONSIN HISTORICAL SOCIETY, IMAGE ID 23433

LEFT: Smoke rising from the third State Capitol building, February 1904. Firefighters' efforts were hampered by the empty University of Wisconsin reservoir and frigid temperatures, and the building was destroyed, except for the north wing, which sustained heavy damage. COURTESY WISCONSIN HISTORICAL SOCIETY, IMAGE ID 1906

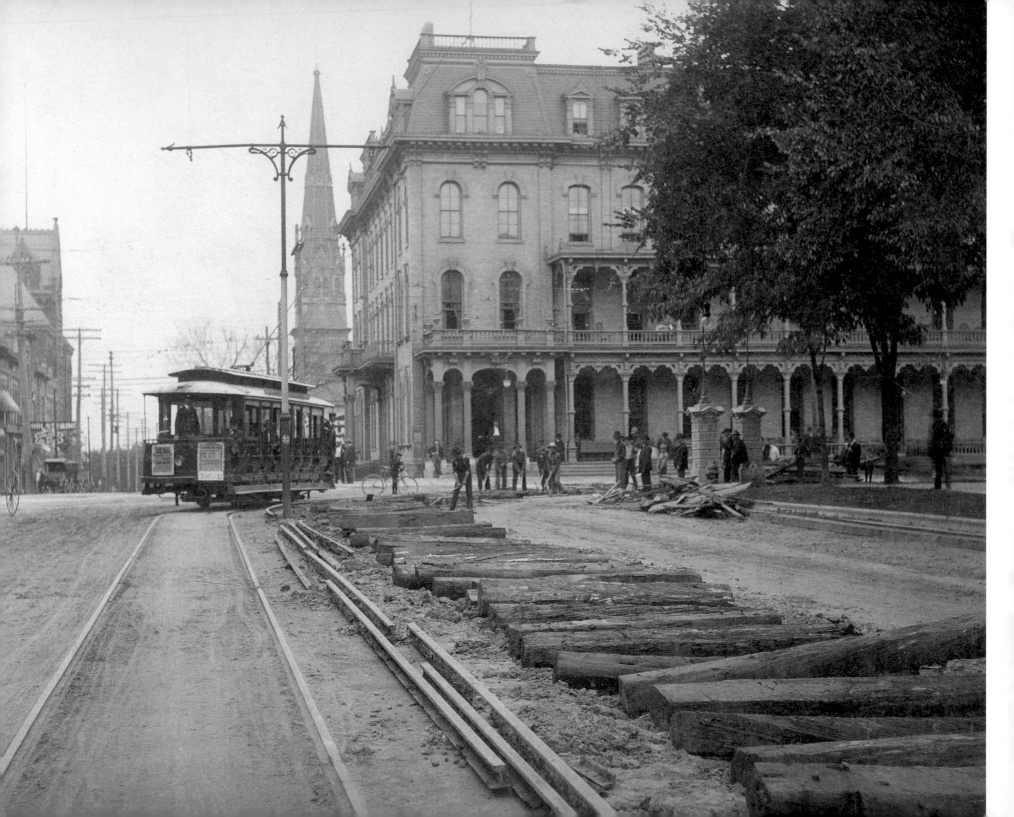

ABOVE: Children playing with a makeshift diving board at Brittingham Bay swimming hole, circa 1904.
COURTESY WISCONSIN HISTORICAL SOCIETY, IMAGE ID 11074

ABOVE LEFT: Rail car passing over the Harrison Street viaduct on the Wingra Park line, circa 1906. The line served the growing suburbs of University Heights, Oakland Heights and Wingra Park. This car had 10 bench seats running across the car and was rated as a 50-passenger car. Such cars were used extensively for transporting crowds back and forth to Forest Hill Cemetery, circus grounds, and for recreational summer rides. COURTESY WISCONSIN HISTORICAL SOCIETY, IMAGE ID 26617

LEFT: Madison Public Library when it was located in City Hall, 2 West Mifflin Street, circa 1905.
COURTESY WISCONSIN HISTORICAL SOCIETY, IMAGE ID 83354

OPPOSITE: Construction of streetcar tracks on Capitol Square at the corner of West Main and South Carroll streets, circa 1905. The Park Hotel and St. Raphael's Catholic Church are in the background.
COURTESY WISCONSIN HISTORICAL SOCIETY, IMAGE ID 24969

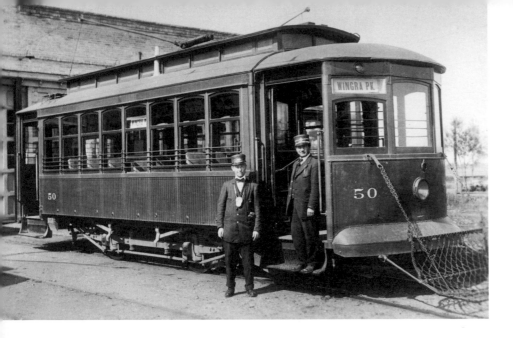

ABOVE: Madison City Railways Co. streetcar No. 50 and its crew, circa 1911. COURTESY WISCONSIN HISTORICAL SOCIETY, IMAGE ID 1827

ABOVE RIGHT: Unloading freight from a Chicago, St. Paul, Minneapolis, and Omaha Railway train at the Madison Depot in 1913. COURTESY WISCONSIN HISTORICAL SOCIETY, IMAGE ID 24347

RIGHT: Construction of the fourth State Capitol building, circa 1911. To the right is the north wing of the third State Capitol that was largely spared from the 1904 fire and used while the other wings were rebuilt. COURTESY WISCONSIN HISTORICAL SOCIETY, IMAGE ID 3482

OPPOSITE: Dedication of the Camp Randall Memorial Arch, June 19, 1912. COURTESY WISCONSIN HISTORICAL SOCIETY, IMAGE ID 11270

ABOVE: Demolition workers in the north wing of the third State Capitol building, 1913. The north wing survived the 1904 fire that destroyed the rest of the building, allowing it to be used for several years during construction of the fourth capitol. COURTESY WISCONSIN HISTORICAL SOCIETY, IMAGE ID 4899

LEFT: The Chicago and Northwestern Railroad Depot on South Blair Street, 1916. COURTESY WISCONSIN STATE JOURNAL

OPPOSITE: Smoke billowing out of the Wisconsin Building onto State Street (left) and North Carroll Street (right) as firemen combat the blaze from both sides, January 13, 1914. The building housed the Commercial National Bank and Keeley's Palace of Sweets, known at the time as "The Pal." COURTESY WISCONSIN HISTORICAL SOCIETY, IMAGE ID 119127

ABOVE: Victory Garden display in the window of John J. Blied & Sons during World War I. Civilians were encouraged to grow vegetables and fruits during wartime to lessen the burden on the national food supply. COURTESY WISCONSIN STATE JOURNAL

LEFT: University of Wisconsin students participating in a machine gun drill in 1918.
COURTESY WISCONSIN STATE JOURNAL

OPPOSITE: Maypole dances on Bascom Hill at the University of Wisconsin, 1916.
COURTESY WISCONSIN HISTORICAL SOCIETY, IMAGE ID 3159

ABOVE: A crowd seeing World War I draftees off to basic training at the Chicago and Northwestern Railroad Depot at the intersection of South Blair and East Wilson Streets, May 25, 1918. COURTESY WISCONSIN HISTORICAL SOCIETY, IMAGE ID 35079

ABOVE RIGHT: Alvin C. Reis of Madison during his service in World War I. During the war, Reis commanded several observation balloon squadrons. He later became a Dane County Circuit Court judge. COURTESY WISCONSIN STATE JOURNAL

RIGHT: Sen. Robert M. La Follette, Sr. (seated turning dial) listening to radio reports of the 1924 presidential election in the Executive Chamber in the State Capitol building. The senator was the Progressive candidate in the election, winning Wisconsin and picking up 16.6 percent of the popular vote. Others, from left: Isabel Bacon La Follette, Mrs. John L. Blaine, Philip Fox La Follette, Governor John J. Blaine, Robert M. La Follette, Jr. COURTESY WISCONSIN HISTORICAL SOCIETY, IMAGE ID 6907

OPPOSITE: University of Wisconsin student cadets learning to repair cars and trucks during World War I. COURTESY WISCONSIN STATE JOURNAL

CHAPTER THREE

THE 1920s AND '30s

The 1920s were most definitely a roaring time in Madison, with that roar reaching a peak on Aug. 27, 1927, when world-famous aviator Charles Lindbergh returned to the city of his college days in his plane, the Spirit of St. Louis, just three months after his trailblazing flight across the Atlantic.

Lindy's visit to Madison was the inspiration later that year for the city to purchase 290 acres of low, flat land along Highway 51 as the future site of a municipal airport. The marshy, wet conditions proved problematic for years, but eventually, with assistance from the Works Progress Administration, the project was completed and the airport opened in 1939.

Like the rest of the nation, Madison also was subjected to the perils of the stock market crash in 1929. On Black Thursday, Oct. 24, 1929, the State Journal's main headline blared: "Five Billions lost in Stocks Slump." The Great Depression was on, and the boom times of the 1920s had vanished.

Along with battling the economy, Madison fought another foe – alcohol – throughout the 1920s and into the early '30s. Near the turn of the century, the city was home to five breweries. But even before Prohibition became the law of the land in 1920, Madison created a series of "saloon-free, dry zones" and eventually banned alcohol sales in 1917.

But the 1930s were not all gloom and doom in Madison. Oscar Mayer & Co. was among many city businesses that thrived during that time.

And like Lindbergh's visit a decade earlier, celebrity came calling again in Madison, first with a visit by baseball slugger Babe Ruth in 1935, just after he retired from his illustrious career with the New York Yankees, and then by a slugger of another type in the late 1930s, heavyweight boxing icon Jack Dempsey.

OPPOSITE: Hearing testing at Emerson School, February 11, 1935. COURTESY WISCONSIN HISTORICAL SOCIETY, IMAGE ID 16074

TOP: Wisconsin State Journal staff, January 1924. COURTESY WISCONSIN STATE JOURNAL

ABOVE: East Side High School graduating class of 1924. COURTESY WISCONSIN HISTORICAL SOCIETY, IMAGE ID 70924

ABOVE RIGHT: National Guardsman Gordon Mott on Spaight Street, circa 1924. COURTESY SUE FITZ GIBBON

RIGHT: Dancers at the Kehl School of Dance, founded by Frederick W. Kehl, circa 1920.
COURTESY WISCONSIN HISTORICAL SOCIETY, IMAGE ID 26184

OPPOSITE: The Jackson home at 415 North Carroll Street, circa 1920. Second from left, holding the toy airplane, is Reginald Jackson Jr., who went on to head the Wisconsin Wing of the Civil Air Patrol. COURTESY WISCONSIN HISTORICAL SOCIETY, IMAGE ID 54343

ABOVE: From left, Central High School cheerleaders "Rudy" Custer, "Monty" Hacker and Frank Custer, March 31, 1929. Rudy and Frank were twins. Frank Custer became a Capital Times Newspaper reporter.
COURTESY WISCONSIN HISTORICAL SOCIETY, IMAGE ID 21339

ABOVE RIGHT: St. Raphael's School class, circa 1929.
COURTESY WISCONSIN HISTORICAL SOCIETY, IMAGE ID 102465

RIGHT: The Strand Theater, 16 East Mifflin Street near the corner of Wisconsin Avenue, August 11, 1927. The marquee advertises "Babe Comes Home" starring Babe Ruth and Anna Q. Nilsson.
COURTESY WISCONSIN HISTORICAL SOCIETY, IMAGE ID 3138

FAR RIGHT: University of Wisconsin student studying in his dorm room, 1925.
COURTESY WISCONSIN HISTORICAL SOCIETY, IMAGE ID 54692

ABOVE: Cars lining up at Pennco filling station at the corner of State and Gorham streets for free oil changes offered during a winter cold snap, January 17, 1927. COURTESY WISCONSIN HISTORICAL SOCIETY, IMAGE ID 6357

LEFT: Charles Lindbergh walking to the hangar at Pennco Field, located south of Lake Monona, following his arrival on Aug. 22, 1927. COURTESY WISCONSIN STATE JOURNAL

ABOVE: Children listening to a radio broadcast at Emerson School, 2421 East Johnson Street, October 1, 1931. COURTESY WISCONSIN HISTORICAL SOCIETY, IMAGE ID 18402

ABOVE LEFT: Streetcar advertisements for the Marx Brothers film "Animal Crackers" playing at the Capitol Theatre, September 6, 1930. COURTESY WISCONSIN HISTORICAL SOCIETY, IMAGE ID 20163

LEFT: Sheriff Fred Simon (right) destroying illegal slot machines, circa 1930s. COURTESY WISCONSIN HISTORICAL SOCIETY, IMAGE ID 67014

OPPOSITE: The Capitol and Orpheum theaters in State Street's 200 block, circa 1929. COURTESY WISCONSIN HISTORICAL SOCIETY, IMAGE ID 3157

ABOVE: Madison boys experimenting with diving equipment, July 13, 1933. From left are Lyell Tullis, Edgar Tullis, Jerry Randall and two unidentified friends.
COURTESY WISCONSIN HISTORICAL SOCIETY, IMAGE ID 17193

RIGHT: Jennie Justo (left) saying goodbye to her mother at 921 Spring Street in the Greenbush neighborhood as she leaves for a long stint in a Milwaukee jail, circa 1931. Known as the "Queen of the Bootleggers" during Prohibition, Justo worked her way through the University of Wisconsin selling bootleg wine before establishing some of the most popular speakeasies around town.
COURTESY WISCONSIN HISTORICAL SOCIETY

OPPOSITE TOP LEFT: Police officer Earl V. Bonner, the shortest man on the Madison police force, and Romain W. York, Jr., the tallest, April 21, 1932. COURTESY WISCONSIN HISTORICAL SOCIETY, IMAGE ID 17955

OPPOSITE TOP RIGHT: Dane County motorcycle police officers with their Harley Davidsons in front of Madison Battery and Tire at 250 State Street, May 16, 1931.
COURTESY WISCONSIN HISTORICAL SOCIETY, IMAGE ID 19219

OPPOSITE BOTTOM LEFT: The Fauerbach Brewery and other businesses along the 600 block of Williamson Street, August 12, 1931. COURTESY WISCONSIN HISTORICAL SOCIETY, IMAGE ID 5008

OPPOSITE BOTTOM RIGHT: Morey Airplane Co. repair shop at Royal Airport south of Lake Monona, May 26, 1932. Howard Morey established the airport as Pennco Field in 1926. This hangar and airplane were lost to a fire a few months after this photo was taken.
COURTESY WISCONSIN HISTORICAL SOCIETY, IMAGE ID 10866

ABOVE: Officers with their new police ambulance in front of the Madison Police Station at 14–16 South Webster Street, November 14, 1934.
COURTESY WISCONSIN HISTORICAL SOCIETY, IMAGE ID 16201

LEFT: East High School football coach A.J. "Hunk" Barrett (center) conversing with two of his players on the practice field, September 6, 1934.
COURTESY WISCONSIN HISTORICAL SOCIETY, IMAGE ID 16356

OPPOSITE: Evangelist W. P. Butler (center left) and the Reverend Joseph Washington (center right) preparing to baptize Lulu Elroy in Lake Monona, June 7, 1933.
COURTESY WISCONSIN HISTORICAL SOCIETY, IMAGE ID 17285

ABOVE: From left, Wisconsin State Journal sports columnist "Roundy" Coughlin and WSJ sports editor Henry McCormick with heavyweight boxing icon Jack Dempsey in Madison, circa late 1930s. COURTESY WISCONSIN STATE JOURNAL

RIGHT: Baseball legend Babe Ruth signing autographs at the Madison depot, October 15, 1935. Ruth had retired from professional baseball earlier that year. COURTESY WISCONSIN HISTORICAL SOCIETY, IMAGE ID 16271

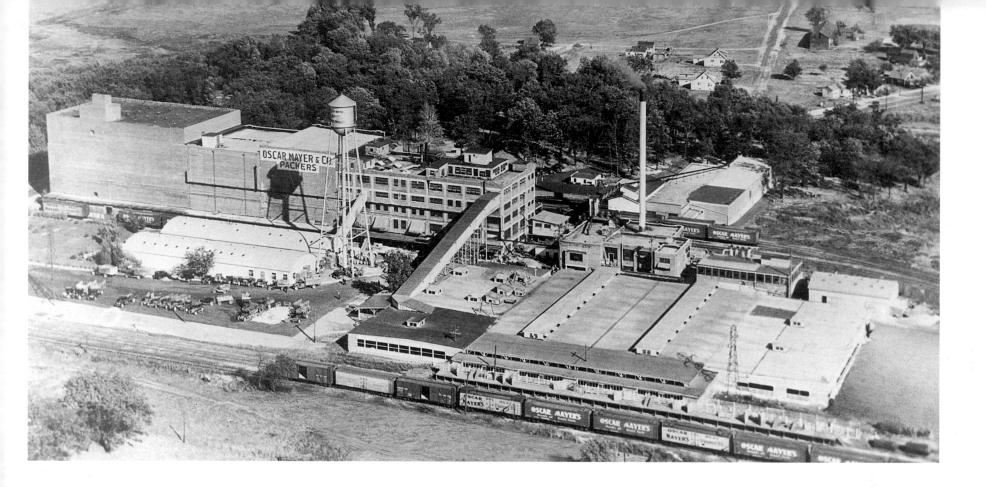

ABOVE: Oscar Mayer & Co. factory, circa 1930s. COURTESY WISCONSIN STATE JOURNAL

LEFT: Disabled veterans who were Forget-Me-Not ice cream bar vendors at 503 State Street, May 17, 1934. The ice cream mix was produced at the University of Wisconsin and the ice cream was manufactured by the Crystal Products Co. at 412 West Gilman Street. WISCONSIN HISTORICAL SOCIETY, IMAGE ID 2042

ABOVE: Second-grade class at Dudgeon School, 3200 Monroe Street, June 5, 1935.
COURTESY WISCONSIN HISTORICAL SOCIETY, IMAGE ID 15880

ABOVE RIGHT: City of Madison recreational volleyball champions, 1935. Front left is Agnes Balk. Back right is Frances Balk. COURTESY SUE FITZ GIBBON

RIGHT: The Valvoline filling station at 999 South Park Street, August 22, 1935. COURTESY WISCONSIN HISTORICAL SOCIETY, IMAGE ID 16691

OPPOSITE: The Fauerbach Brewery at 651-654 Williamson Street, circa 1935. COURTESY WISCONSIN STATE JOURNAL

ABOVE: Chicago and Northwestern Railroad crossing maintenance near the 100 block of South Blair Street, October 27, 1936.
COURTESY WISCONSIN HISTORICAL SOCIETY, IMAGE ID 3853

RIGHT: The Orpheum Theater in the 200 block of State Street, January 24, 1936. The marquee advertises orchestra leader Shep Fields on stage and "Kind Lady" starring Aline MacMahon on screen.
COURTESY WISCONSIN HISTORICAL SOCIETY, IMAGE ID 6415

OPPOSITE TOP LEFT: A Kennedy-Mansfield Dairy wagon in front of the Parkway Theater at 6-10 West Mifflin Street, March 13, 1936. Barney Miller, left, is feeding hay to "Ned," the oldest dairy horse in service at the time. COURTESY WISCONSIN HISTORICAL SOCIETY, IMAGE ID 15545

OPPOSITE BOTTOM LEFT: Switchboard operators referencing rotary directory files at Wisconsin Telephone Co., 17 South Fairchild Street, June 25, 1937. COURTESY WISCONSIN HISTORICAL SOCIETY, IMAGE ID 15068

OPPOSITE RIGHT: A sales clerk demonstrating an automobile heater to a customer at Halperin Auto Parts, 209 South Park Street, October 20, 1937. COURTESY WISCONSIN HISTORICAL SOCIETY, IMAGE ID 14887

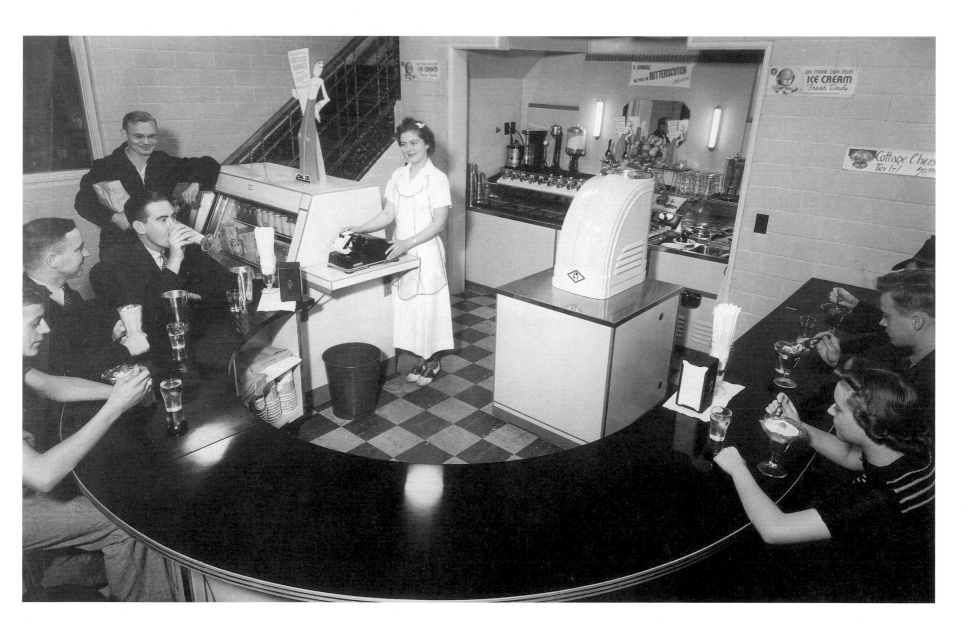

ABOVE: Bancroft Dairy Fountain Room, 1010 South Park Street. September 20, 1937. COURTESY WISCONSIN HISTORICAL SOCIETY, IMAGE ID 2040

OPPOSITE: Students with a AAA dual-control training Pontiac at East High School, 2222 East Washington Avenue, October 27, 1938. COURTESY WISCONSIN HISTORICAL SOCIETY, IMAGE ID 14624

ABOVE: Oscar Mayer & Co. casing department employees, 910 Mayer Avenue, October 17, 1939. COURTESY WISCONSIN HISTORICAL SOCIETY, IMAGE ID 14344

ABOVE RIGHT: Wisconsin Auto License Bureau Card Typing Department, 16-20 E. Doty Street, May 17, 1939. COURTESY WISCONSIN HISTORICAL SOCIETY, IMAGE ID 14424

RIGHT: Sixth-grade class at Dudgeon School, 3200 Monroe Street, June 7, 1939. COURTESY WISCONSIN HISTORICAL SOCIETY, IMAGE ID 14407

OPPOSITE: Frank Brothers grocery store, 609-613 University Avenue, April 7, 1939. COURTESY WISCONSIN HISTORICAL SOCIETY, IMAGE ID 14463

ADMISSION
ADULTS 40¢
CHILDREN 25¢
UNDER 12
DRINK
Coca-Cola
SWING
COCONUT
MINT

CHAPTER FOUR

THE 1940s

Having survived the economic challenges of the Great Depression in the late 1920s and '30s, war once again became the overarching theme in Madison in the early 1940s.

By 1939, the situation in Europe was at a boiling point. Adolph Hitler sent troops into Poland on September 1, and Britain delivered an ultimatum to Germany. For the next six years, war would dominate the headlines of the Wisconsin State Journal.

Just over a year later, on October 26, 1940, a crew of workers at the newspaper labored all day to ready the lists of numbers for the local draftees, so they would know how they fared in the United States' first peace-time draft lottery three days later.

Among Wisconsin's war heroes: John H. Bradley of Antigo, a Marine who would gain fame as one of the six men who raised the U.S. flag on Mount Suribachi 1945. Joe Rosenthal's photograph of that epic moment became one of the most iconic images from World War II.

A more local but similarly iconic image was created by State Journal photographer Arthur M. Vinje on August 14, 1945, on a Downtown Madison street. Vinje captured a shot of newsboy Bernard Ehrman celebrating Victory Over Japan Day with Navy Seaman Tom Teeley, who was passing through Madison after 17 months in the Pacific theater. The photo of young Ehrman and Navy man Teeley both beaming while Ehrman hawked "extra" editions of the State Journal became a nostalgic reminder of the times.

Of the 120,000 Wisconsin soldiers who served in World War II, likely the best known was William "Billy" Mitchell, after whom Milwaukee's General Mitchell International Airport is named. Mitchell played a prominent role in the war as commander of the U.S. Army Air Service.

OPPOSITE: Jane Spencer handing a soda to Peter Weiss while Lucille Madigan and Helen Topp look over the selection of records in the warming room and snack bar at the Madison Figure Skating Club's new indoor skating arena at Truax Field, January 12, 1949. COURTESY WISCONSIN HISTORICAL SOCIETY, IMAGE ID 56843

ABOVE: The Chicago and Northwestern Railroad station and Lake View Hotel at the corner of East Wilson and South Blair streets, circa 1940. COURTESY WISCONSIN HISTORICAL SOCIETY, IMAGE ID 6890

LEFT: Bridge over the creek between Lake Wingra and Lake Monona, Vilas Park, circa 1940. COURTESY JANET COOPER

OPPOSITE TOP LEFT: Product demonstration in the Schultz Tire and Battery Service workshop at 1336 Regent Street, December 27, 1940. COURTESY WISCONSIN HISTORICAL SOCIETY, IMAGE ID 14122

OPPOSITE TOP RIGHT: Girl Scouts at Camp Indianola on Lake Mendota with the Madison skyline in the background, October 10, 1941. COURTESY WISCONSIN HISTORICAL SOCIETY, IMAGE ID 13807

OPPOSITE BOTTOM: R.F. Lease and Co. fleet of floor sanders at 209 East Main Street, November 9, 1941. COURTESY WISCONSIN HISTORICAL SOCIETY, IMAGE ID 13882

ABOVE: A Madison youth string quartet, March 1941. From left are Jane Parkin, Janet Hart, Nancy Hart, and Polly Richardson. COURTESY JANET COOPER

RIGHT: 76-year old Henry L. Krehl, believed to the be city's oldest soda jerk at the time, working the fountain at his brother August W. "Doc" Krehl's drug store, 408 E. Wilson Street, October 10, 1944. The young soda jerks were off fighting in World War II. COURTESY WISCONSIN HISTORICAL SOCIETY, IMAGE ID 40918

OPPOSITE TOP LEFT: Madison wrestler Jimmy Demetral (right) teaching Officer Robert O'Brien to do an "airplane spin" toss on Officer Keith Ackley, February 2, 1944. 55 Madison Police Department officers were enrolled in a five-week judo course. COURTESY WISCONSIN HISTORICAL SOCIETY, IMAGE ID 38092

OPPOSITE TOP RIGHT: Oscar Mayer & Co. switchboard operator, January 19, 1944. COURTESY WISCONSIN HISTORICAL SOCIETY, IMAGE ID 13487

OPPOSITE BOTTOM LEFT: Four generations in 1945. From left: Englebert C. Schlimgen, Eleanor Rowley, Lawrence G. Schlimgen, infant Penny Rowley. COURTESY KATHY SCHLIMGEN

OPPOSITE BOTTOM RIGHT: Lorraine Gray and Mrs. Mildred Lewis on the production line at the Ruben-Mallory plant, a division of Ray-O-Vac located in the 1400 block of East Washington Avenue, November 1945. The plant manufactured batteries for military walkie-talkies during World War II. COURTESY WISCONSIN HISTORICAL SOCIETY, IMAGE ID 41516

ABOVE: Four-year-old Josie Donovan celebrating at Capitol Square on Victory Over Japan Day, August 14, 1945. Her father was a prisoner of war in the Pacific and hadn't been heard from in 18 months at that point.
COURTESY WISCONSIN STATE JOURNAL

RIGHT: Wisconsin State Journal newsboy Bernard Ehrman celebrating Victory Over Japan Day with Seaman Tom Teeley, who was passing through Madison after 17 months in the Pacific, August 14, 1945.
COURTESY WISCONSIN STATE JOURNAL

ABOVE: Monona Avenue near Doty Street looking south toward the Capitol during a January 1947 snowstorm.
COURTESY WISCONSIN STATE JOURNAL

ABOVE LEFT: The "Court of Honor" for the University of Wisconsin Military Ball, April 23, 1947. From left: Suzanne Johnson (Kappa Kappa Gamma sorority), Barbara Ross (Tower View House), Gloria Damon (Anderson House), Eileen Freud (Cochrane House) and Lois Lauridsen, (Delta Delta Delta sorority). COURTESY WISCONSIN HISTORICAL SOCIETY, IMAGE ID 46904

LEFT: Postal clerk Matt Morrell stacking parcels of holiday mail at the Madison Post Office on December 18, 1947.
COURTESY WISCONSIN HISTORICAL SOCIETY, IMAGE ID 49456

ABOVE: Lake Mendota pier during an intercollegiate Hoofer invitational regatta, July 17, 1948. From left: Don Williams, a University of Wisconsin senior and member of Hoofers Club; Edward Bainbridge, commodore of the University of Michigan Yacht Club; and Paul Moore, president of the Midwest Collegiate Yachting association.
COURTESY WISCONSIN HISTORICAL SOCIETY, IMAGE ID 53426

ABOVE RIGHT: Crowd watching the U.S. Army 32nd Division marching along East Main Street during the Wisconsin Centennial Parade, May 29, 1948.
COURTESY WISCONSIN HISTORICAL SOCIETY, IMAGE ID 52650

RIGHT: The eighth-grade graduating class of St. Raphael Catholic School, 216 West Main Street, June 9, 1948.
COURTESY WISCONSIN HISTORICAL SOCIETY, IMAGE ID 52689

OPPOSITE: Mt. Zion Baptist Church congregation in front of the church at 548 West Johnson Street, June 6, 1948.
COURTESY WISCONSIN HISTORICAL SOCIETY, IMAGE ID 52695

ABOVE: Square dancers performing at the Madison Community Center, March 27, 1949.
COURTESY WISCONSIN HISTORICAL SOCIETY, IMAGE ID 58475

LEFT: From left, Jeanne Faber, Bebe Shopp (Miss America 1948), Suzanne Wheeler and Anne Barber riding in the back of a convertible, April 2, 1949. Shopp was brought to Madison to reign as queen of the U.W. Faville-Gilman-Noyes houses formal Tophatter Dance in the Park Hotel. COURTESY WISCONSIN HISTORICAL SOCIETY, IMAGE ID 58509

OPPOSITE: A visiting choir with members of Mt. Zion Baptist Church, 548 West Johnson Street, June 6, 1948. COURTESY WISCONSIN HISTORICAL SOCIETY, IMAGE ID 55741

CHAPTER FIVE

THE 1950s

The 1950s started with a flourish in Madison when President Harry S. Truman came to town in May 1950. Among other stops during his visit to Madison, Truman participated in the laying of the cornerstone of Filene House, then the international headquarters of the Credit Union National Association, at 1617 Sherman Avenue.

Meanwhile, Madison, like the rest of the nation, generally basked in peace and prosperity during the 1950s. The population grew, recreation opportunities abounded and the post-World War II and pre-Vietnam era was largely calm and lacking in turmoil.

But no city is without controversy for a decade, and among Madison's disagreements in the '50s was what do with Frank Lloyd Wright's vision for what would later become Monona Terrace.

Wright, already famous, flamboyant and regarded as an architectural genius, picked up on the plans of early city planner John Nolen and first unveiled his "dream civic center"

in November 1938. It included city and county offices, a jail, railroad depot and a boat facility as part of a semi-circular building at the foot of Monona Avenue and extending over the lake.

Initially, the project met with favor, and in 1941 Madison voters approved by a 2-1 margin two referendums to build the $750,000 complex. Soon after, Wright revised the project and reintroduced it as a civic center. However, U.S. entry into World War II tabled the discussion.

In the post-war years, Wright's vision faced fierce opposition and sparked nasty public battles throughout the 1950s. Then, on April 9, 1959, Wright died in Arizona, just two months shy of his 92nd birthday.

Mayor Ivan Nestingen noted then that Wright's death would cause "some delay" in the Monona Terrace project. Indeed. It was almost 40 years later, in 1997, when Monona Terrace finally opened its doors.

OPPOSITE: North Central Airlines DC-3 airplane flying over the Madison isthmus in 1952. COURTESY WISCONSIN HISTORICAL SOCIETY, IMAGE ID 1922

ABOVE: Madison Bus Co. employee Roger Drouin, 1950.
COURTESY JERRIE MURPHY

ABOVE MIDDLE: Two sisters boarding a train bound for out-of-state colleges on August 23, 1950. Mary Clare Koltes (left) was transferring to Rollins College in Florida while her younger sister, Lucia, was a freshman at Maryville College in Missouri. COURTESY WISCONSIN HISTORICAL SOCIETY, IMAGE ID 66923

ABOVE RIGHT: Badger School eighth-grade class, 1951-1952. Front row, from left: Barbara Normington, Irene Pfister, Rosalie Kaether, Mary Graves, Joanne Schuepbach, Stella Middleton. Back row: Mr. Hoesly, Pearl, Clifford Olson, John Olson, Marvin Bjornstad, Tom P., Eugene Bjornstad. COURTESY FITCHBURG HISTORICAL SOCIETY

RIGHT: The F.W. Woolworth building at the corner of East Main Street and Monona Avenue (Martin Luther King Boulevard), circa early 1950s. COURTESY WISCONSIN STATE JOURNAL

ABOVE: Mineral Point Soap Box Derby participants marching the course, 1950.

COURTESY WISCONSIN STATE JOURNAL

LEFT: Corporal Albert Griffin, a soldier from Milwaukee wounded in the Korean War, standing with Gov. Oscar Rennebohm at the freedom bell during United Nations Day ceremonies at the State Capitol, October 24, 1950.

COURTESY WISCONSIN HISTORICAL SOCIETY, IMAGE ID 68080

BELOW: President Harry S. Truman moments after formally laying the cornerstone of CUNA's Filene House at 1617 Sherman Avenue on May 14, 1950.

COURTESY WISCONSIN STATE JOURNAL

ABOVE: The pigeon hole parking ramp, at the corner of Wisconsin Avenue and East Dayton Street, behind Manchester's Department Store, 1954. COURTESY WISCONSIN STATE JOURNAL

ABOVE RIGHT: Wisconsin State Journal editor Roy L. Matson boarding a plane at the start of a 25,000-mile air tour of Europe and the Near East sponsored by the United States Department of Defense, January 15, 1952. The flight attendant is Miss Brosnahn. COURTESY WISCONSIN HISTORICAL SOCIETY, IMAGE ID 73656

RIGHT: Bob Bell (left) using a soldering iron in the electronics workshop at the Naval Reserve Training Center at 1046 East Washington Avenue in Madison, August 31, 1954. Looking on are Jim Karch, Bob Hausgard and Don Carey. COURTESY WISCONSIN HISTORICAL SOCIETY, IMAGE ID 88366

OPPOSITE: Madison West and Onalaska high schools during the opening game of the WIAA state basketball tournament, March 15, 1951. COURTESY WISCONSIN HISTORICAL SOCIETY, IMAGE ID 70024

ABOVE: Frank Lloyd Wright receiving an honorary Doctorate of Fine Arts degree from the University of Wisconsin during commencement, June 1955. COURTESY WISCONSIN STATE JOURNAL

LEFT: Frank Lloyd Wright and Mayor George Foster discussing the Monona Terrace model at City Hall, February 7, 1955. COURTESY WISCONSIN STATE JOURNAL

OPPOSITE: Class A quarter-mile race during the Wisconsin State High Cchool track meet at Camp Randall Stadium, May 29, 1954. The winner of this race was Jesse Nixon of Milwaukee Lincoln, running at far right. COURTESY WISCONSIN HISTORICAL SOCIETY, IMAGE ID 87302

ABOVE: Employees of the Gisholt Machine Co. on East Washington Avenue, 1955. COURTESY WISCONSIN STATE JOURNAL

RIGHT: Madison Royalettes cocktail and supper party in the Gold Room of the Playdium, February 13, 1955. Royalettes president, Mrs. Mary Cooper (Grimes), is seated in the center. COURTESY WISCONSIN HISTORICAL SOCIETY, IMAGE ID 90724

OPPOSITE: Downtown Madison looking north from above Lake Monona up Monona Avenue (Martin Luther King Boulevard), circa 1950s. COURTESY WISCONSIN STATE JOURNAL

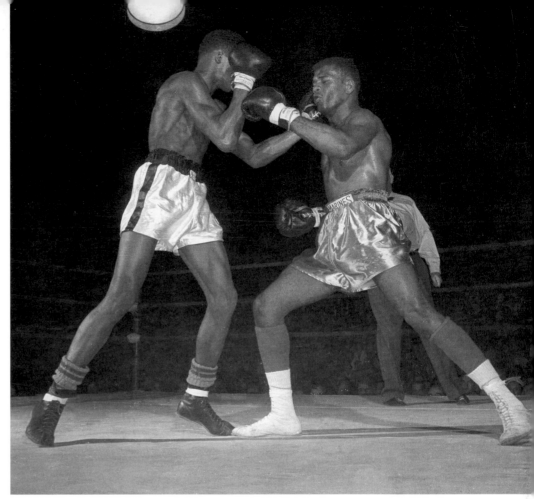

ABOVE: Cassius Clay (later Muhammad Ali) in the white trucks at left fighting Amos Johnson in the light heavyweight final of the Pan-American Games boxing trials at the University of Wisconsin Field House, April 30, 1959. Johnson won the bout and went on to win the gold medal at the Chicago games. COURTESY WISCONSIN HISTORICAL SOCIETY, IMAGE ID 10122

ABOVE LEFT: Schuepbach Farm off East Clayton Road with a view of the State Capitol, 1958.
COURTESY JOANNE SCHUEPBACH JENSEN

LEFT: The Chicago, Milwaukee, and St. Paul Railroad station, roundhouse, and yard at the intersection of West Washington Avenue and Regent Street, circa 1956.
COURTESY WISCONSIN HISTORICAL SOCIETY, IMAGE ID 4901

OPPOSITE: Monona Hotel and Indian Room bar on Monona Avenue (Martin Luther King Boulevard) off Capitol Square, August 7, 1956. COURTESY WISCONSIN STATE JOURNAL

ABOVE: Cars turning from South Pinckney Street onto West Mifflin Street on the Capitol Square, August 1959. Businesses include Madison Hotel, Victor Music, Woldenberg's and Moseley's. COURTESY WISCONSIN STATE JOURNAL

ABOVE RIGHT: WHA-TV studios broadcast, March 19, 1958.
COURTESY WISCONSIN STATE JOURNAL

RIGHT: East High School basketball players celebrating their 1958 state championship. Second from right is Pat Richter, who went on to become a nine-time letterman at the University of Wisconsin, an eight-year veteran of the NFL with the Washington Redskins and UW's athletic director.
COURTESY PAT RICHTER FAMILY, WISCONSIN STATE JOURNAL

ABOVE: Vice President Richard Nixon speaking outside the State Capitol, October 1958.
COURTESY WISCONSIN STATE JOURNAL

LEFT: Teenage supporters of the proposed Frank Lloyd Wright Monona Terrace Auditorium, attending the opening of the Monona Terrace Pavilion, 1958. From left: Jane Ragsdale, Jean Kruger, Linda Kloe, Tom Jambols. COURTESY WISCONSIN STATE JOURNAL

CHAPTER SIX

THE 1960s

Rolling from the relative calm of the 1950s into the turbulent 1960s, Madison would soon become a focal point of the nation's unrest – and particularly the anti-Vietnam War movement – as protesters, non-violent and violent alike, found traction in the late '60s.

Long before the anti-war disturbances put Madison on the national protest map, presidential politics came to town. On October 23, 1960, Sen. John F. Kennedy drew a packed crowd to the University of Wisconsin Field House while campaigning for president. Meanwhile, on Nov. 7, 1960, the eve of the presidential election that was won by Kennedy, vice president Richard Nixon and his wife, Pat, made a last-minute campaign stop in Madison.

Just over three years later, Madison mourned with the rest of the nation upon learning that Kennedy had been assassinated in Dallas. Some 800 people attended a Pontifical Requiem Mass given by Bishop Jerome J. Hastrich at St. Raphael's Cathedral in Madison on November 25, 1963, three days after the 46-year-old president was slain.

By the mid-1960s, UW-Madison, like many other college campuses, was fully embroiled in the anti-war movement. In October 1965, police arrested 11 people who took part in a sit-in at Truax Field. More arrests came in February 1967 following protests against Dow Chemical, a manufacturer of napalm.

But it wasn't until October 1967 that Madison witnessed violence between protesters and police. On October 18, protesters and police clashed at the old Commerce building. "Nightsticks were the authorities' main weapon," according to a State Journal story about the protest.

That day changed the dynamic in Madison. Protests grew more violent, activists became more radical, and nightsticks and tear gas became routine. All that set a dark stage for what was to come: a fatal bombing in August 1970.

OPPOSITE: University of Wisconsin students marching down State Street in support of the school's African-American community, February 16, 1969.
COURTESY WISCONSIN STATE JOURNAL

ABOVE: Madison Bank and Trust Co. President John Shiels (left) and Vice President Edwin Petterle looking over a drawing of the proposed Monona Terrace building "dance hall" at one of five Madison business establishments displaying similar drawings, circa 1960. COURTESY WISCONSIN STATE JOURNAL

ABOVE LEFT: Vice President Richard Nixon and his wife, Pat, making a last-minute campaign stop in Madison on November 7, 1960, the eve of the presidential election. COURTESY WISCONSIN STATE JOURNAL

LEFT: Wesley Peters (left), Chief Architect of the Frank Lloyd Wright Foundation, and Mayor Ivan A. Nestingen going over the latest plans for the Monona Terrace Civic Center project, circa 1960. COURTESY WISCONSIN STATE JOURNAL

OPPOSITE TOP LEFT: Young John F. Kennedy supporters outside the University of Wisconsin Field House where the senator campaigned for president, October 24, 1960. COURTESY WISCONSIN STATE JOURNAL

OPPOSITE BOTTOM LEFT: Gisholt Machine Tool Manufacturing Co. plant on East Washington Avenue, August 30, 1962. COURTESY WISCONSIN STATE JOURNAL

OPPOSITE RIGHT: Senator John F. Kennedy campaigning for president at the University of Wisconsin Field House, October 23, 1960. COURTESY WISCONSIN STATE JOURNAL

ABOVE: University of Wisconsin cheerleaders celebrating the return of the football team from the 1963 Rose Bowl. The Badgers fell to the University of Southern California Trojans 42-37. COURTESY WISCONSIN STATE JOURNAL

RIGHT: State Street from the Capitol grounds, circa 1960s.
COURTESY WISCONSIN STATE JOURNAL

ABOVE: A Wisconsin State Journal paperboy, circa early 1960s. COURTESY WISCONSIN STATE JOURNAL

ABOVE LEFT: Pontifical Requiem Mass given by Bishop Jerome J. Hastrich at St. Raphael's Cathedral following the assassination of President John F. Kennedy, November 25, 1963. Some 800 people attended the service, which included a sermon by Father Howard Finnegan. COURTESY WISCONSIN STATE JOURNAL

LEFT: Christmas decorations going up on State Street, circa early 1960s. COURTESY WISCONSIN STATE JOURNAL

FAR LEFT: Comedian Bob Hope after entertaining the Homecoming crowd at halftime of a University of Wisconsin Badgers football game against Ohio State at Camp Randall Stadium, October 1965. COURTESY WISCONSIN STATE JOURNAL

RIGHT: University of Wisconsin students protesting the Vietnam War on State Street, November 6, 1968. COURTESY WISCONSIN STATE JOURNAL

OPPOSITE TOP LEFT: University of Wisconsin students protesting the Vietnam War in 1967. COURTESY WISCONSIN STATE JOURNAL

OPPOSITE BOTTOM LEFT: Madison's Eighth Ward Alderman Paul Soglin with his two dogs walking with picketers in an anti-war demonstration in front of the Loraine Hotel, the site of a speech by U.S. Draft Director Lewis B. Hershey, May 1968. COURTESY WISCONSIN STATE JOURNAL

OPPOSITE RIGHT: The Rev. Robert Trobaugh leading a prayer of hope at a University of Wisconsin student vigil on Bascom Hill on October 22, 1967, after the Dow Chemical rioting. COURTESY WISCONSIN STATE JOURNAL

ABOVE: Burgerville, a popular teen hangout on State Street where burgers cost 22 cents, July 1969. COURTESY WISCONSIN STATE JOURNAL

ABOVE RIGHT: In diving suits, from left, Charles Campbell, Travis Brann and Phil Sharrow following their first dive on soul and R&B star Otis Redding's Beechcraft H18 aircraft, December 1967. COURTESY WISCONSIN STATE JOURNAL

RIGHT: John Nolen Drive under construction, July 27, 1967. COURTESY WISCONSIN STATE JOURNAL

OPPOSITE: The wreckage of soul and R&B star Otis Redding's Beechcraft H18 aircraft being pulled out of Lake Monona in December 1967. The plane crashed in poor weather on December 10, killing Redding, fellow musicians Matthew Kelly, Jimmy King, Phalon Jones, Ronnie Caldwell, Carl Cunningham, and pilot Richard Fraser. COURTESY WISCONSIN STATE JOURNAL

ABOVE: National Guardsmen with fixed bayonets confronting students during February 1969 protests at the University of Wisconsin. COURTESY WISCONSIN STATE JOURNAL

ABOVE RIGHT: University of Wisconsin student protesters demonstrating at Bascom Hill in support of the school's African-American community, February 12, 1969. COURTESY WISCONSIN STATE JOURNAL

RIGHT: An altercation during University of Wisconsin student protests in support of the school's African-American community, February 12, 1969. COURTESY WISCONSIN STATE JOURNAL

ABOVE: University of Wisconsin students march in support of African-American student rights, February 14, 1969. COURTESY WISCONSIN STATE JOURNAL

ABOVE LEFT: Chief of Police Ralph Hanson (right) during the University of Wisconsin student protests in support of African-American student rights, February 12, 1969. COURTESY WISCONSIN STATE JOURNAL

LEFT: Protesters on the University of Wisconsin campus block the path of a National Guard jeep in 1969. COURTESY WISCONSIN STATE JOURNAL

CHAPTER SEVEN

THE 1970s, '80s AND '90s

The post-1960s era got off to a horrifying start in Madison when anti-war protesters detonated a home-made bomb – fertilizer and fuel oil packed inside a stolen Ford Econoline van – outside Sterling Hall on the UW-Madison campus in the early morning hours of August 24, 1970.

The perpetrators – brothers Karl and Dwight Armstrong, along with David Fine and Leo Burt – intended to blow up the Army Mathematics Research Center on the upper floors of Sterling Hall. The bomb went off at 3:42 a.m., and Robert Faschnact, a 33-year-old physics researcher working overnight in the basement of the building, was killed.

The Armstrong brothers and Fine were captured and served prison sentences. Burt has never been found.

Meanwhile, Paul Soglin, who gained notoriety as an anti-establishment voice in Madison, vaulted from his seat on the City Council to his first term as mayor in April 1973. Madison residents likely wouldn't have guessed then that Soglin would be elected mayor multiple times over four decades, including his most recent re-election in spring 2015.

The mid-1970s ushered in numerous "footprint" changes to the UW-Madison campus, including construction of the Library Mall that replaced lower State Street. Other "moments in time" from this era:

- The first installation of a faux Statue of Liberty barely jutting out from a frozen Lake Monona came in February 1979, engineered by the Pail and Shovel Party at UW-Madison, headed by Leon Varjian and Jim Mallon. Their stunt gained national attention, and the idea perseveres even today.
- The inaugural concert in the Oscar Mayer Theatre was held February 23, 1980.
- The Henry Vilas Zoo expanded in the 1980s, adding an elephant and two polar bears. In 1991, twin polar bears orphaned in Alaska came to Vilas Zoo, and fund-raising for the cubs also helped pay for a new $450,000 herpetarium.
- Monona Terrace opened its doors on July 18, 1997, nearly 60 years after famed architect Frank Lloyd Wright first proposed the idea.

OPPOSITE: Wisconsin State Journal pressmen looking over the final product at the press on South Carroll Street, 1975. COURTESY WISCONSIN STATE JOURNAL

ABOVE: The Capitol Theater advertising "The Heartbreak Kid" and "Robin Hood," circa 1973. COURTESY WISCONSIN STATE JOURNAL

LEFT: University of Wisconsin student demonstrators walking up State Street to the Capitol to protest the Vietnam War in April 1972. COURTESY WISCONSIN STATE JOURNAL

FAR LEFT: Mayor Paul Soglin during the first day of his mayoral career, April 1973. COURTESY WISCONSIN STATE JOURNAL

OPPOSITE: National Guardsmen outside Bascom Hall on the University of Wisconsin campus during student protests of the escalation of the war in Cambodia, May 7, 1970. COURTESY WISCONSIN STATE JOURNAL

ABOVE: The construction of the Library Mall that replaced lower State Street, September 1975. COURTESY WISCONSIN STATE JOURNAL

ABOVE RIGHT: State Street from the Capitol grounds, January 31, 1974. COURTESY WISCONSIN STATE JOURNAL

BELOW RIGHT: Wisconsin State Journal newsroom, South Carroll Street, 1975. Men in foreground, from left: Fred Sacksteder, Ward Remington, Cliff Behnke, Peter Fox. COURTESY WISCONSIN STATE JOURNAL

OPPOSITE LEFT: The Library Mall, State Street and the Capitol from Bascom Hill, September 1976. COURTESY WISCONSIN STATE JOURNAL

OPPOSITE TOP RIGHT: Monona shoreline, future site of the Monona Terrace Convention Center, circa 1970s. COURTESY WISCONSIN STATE JOURNAL

OPPOSITE BOTTOM RIGHT: Madison firefighters battling the blaze following the protest bombing of Sterling Hall at the University of Wisconsin, August 24, 1970. Sterling Hall held the Army-funded Army Mathematics Research Center. The bombing killed one and injured three. COURTESY WISCONSIN STATE JOURNAL

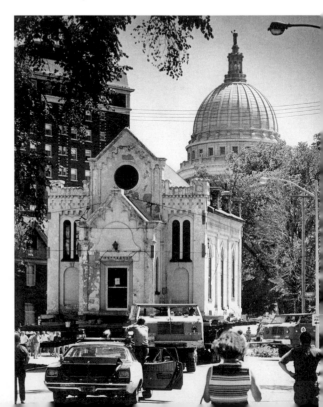

ABOVE: Statue of Liberty installation on the ice of Lake Mendota behind the Memorial Union, February 1979. The stunt was the work of the whimsical Pail & Shovel Party headed by Leon Varjian and Jim Mallon and garnered national attention. Mallon went on to become executive producer of Mystery Science Theater 3000 television program. COURTESY WISCONSIN STATE JOURNAL

ABOVE LEFT: Milwaukee Railroad employee Ralph "Dugan" Keppler, September 1978. COURTESY WISCONSIN STATE JOURNAL

LEFT: California Gov. Edmund Brown Jr. appearing at the Capitol in a live television program directed by Francis Ford Coppola, March 28 1980. COURTESY WISCONSIN STATE JOURNAL

OPPOSITE TOP LEFT: Mount Horeb High School students helping clear broken limbs on North Second Street following an ice storm in March 1976. COURTESY WISCONSIN STATE JOURNAL

OPPOSITE TOP RIGHT: First phase of the Library Mall at the base of State Street, 1970s. COURTESY WISCONSIN STATE JOURNAL

OPPOSITE BOTTOM LEFT: State Street, November 12, 1980. COURTESY WISCONSIN STATE JOURNAL

OPPOSITE BOTTOM RIGHT: The Gates of Heaven synagogue being moved through Madison streets on July 17, 1971. COURTESY WISCONSIN STATE JOURNAL

ABOVE: University of Wisconsin student Leon Varjian leading a boom box parade down State Street on June 2, 1980. Varjian, vice president of the Wisconsin Student Association, helped orchestrate some of the biggest stunts on campus in the late 1970s and early 1980s. COURTESY WISCONSIN STATE JOURNAL

ABOVE RIGHT: Kehl Dance Studio at 223 E. Mifflin Street, 1980. Fourth generation Kehl dancers are in costume for the 100th anniversary celebration performance.
COURTESY JO JEAN KEHL JANUS / KEHL SCHOOL OF DANCE

RIGHT: Downtown, 1980. COURTESY WISCONSIN STATE JOURNAL

FAR RIGHT: Bucky Badger and University of Wisconsin cheerleaders in the 1978 Homecoming parade. COURTESY WISCONSIN STATE JOURNAL

OPPOSITE: The inaugural concert in the Oscar Mayer Theatre on February 23, 1980. It had been the historic Capital Theatre, which opened in 1928. COURTESY WISCONSIN STATE JOURNAL

ABOVE: Willy Street Fair parade, September 25, 1981. COURTESY WISCONSIN STATE JOURNAL

ABOVE LEFT: Flooding at Mifflin and Blount streets, June 15, 1981. COURTESY WISCONSIN STATE JOURNAL

LEFT: Runners participate in the Syttende Mai run, a race between Madison and Stoughton, honoring Norwegian Independence Day, May 18, 1981. COURTESY WISCONSIN STATE JOURNAL

OPPOSITE RIGHT: The manhunt for escaped prisoner Samuel Suggs in 1981. COURTESY WISCONSIN STATE JOURNAL

OPPOSITE TOP LEFT: University of Wisconsin Police Chief Ralph Hanson talking with student protesters during a demonstration against the Central Intelligence Agency on campus, April 1985. COURTESY WISCONSIN STATE JOURNAL

OPPOSITE BOTTOM LEFT: State Street Infirmary Tavern fire at 449 State Street, August 22, 1985. COURTESY WISCONSIN STATE JOURNAL

ABOVE: The Library Mall at the base of State Street, January 1985.
COURTESY WISCONSIN STATE JOURNAL

FAR RIGHT: Terry Wilson of Madison Area Technical College rising to the rim, February 18, 1987. COURTESY WISCONSIN STATE JOURNAL

RIGHT: Anglican Archbishop Desmond Tutu of South Africa hugging an audience member following his sermon at Mt. Zion Baptist Church in May 1988.
COURTESY WISCONSIN STATE JOURNAL

ABOVE: Former Republican Wisconsin Governor Lee S. Dreyfus meeting a Ringling Brothers and Barnum & Bailey Circus elephant, circa 1986. COURTESY WISCONSIN STATE JOURNAL

ABOVE LEFT: The Ringling Brothers and Barnum & Bailey Circus staging an impromptu elephant parade Downtown before heading down John Nolen Drive to the Dane County Memorial Coliseum, September 5, 1986. COURTESY WISCONSIN STATE JOURNAL

LEFT: Children watching Madison Muskies baseball from the free seats, May 6, 1987. COURTESY WISCONSIN STATE JOURNAL

ABOVE: Marissa Potter, 12, of Waunakee in her "Pink Cadillac" racing against Dan Krausman, 16, of Madison in a soap box derby race in July 1992.
COURTESY WISCONSIN STATE JOURNAL

RIGHT: Shon Cooper, 12, playing with leaves while helping a friend on South Mills Street, circa 1993.
COURTESY MARY LANGENFELD

FAR RIGHT: From left, Alexis Shipp, Jennifer Davis and Candace Shipp trick-or-treating on Langdon Street as part of a safe Halloween event for children sponsored by University of Wisconsin fraternities and sororities, October 31, 1996. COURTESY WISCONSIN STATE JOURNAL

ABOVE: A young boy helping a mail carrier on his rounds on Madison's East Side, circa 1992. COURTESY MARY LANGENFELD

LEFT: A member of the Hare Krishna sect talks with some punk rockers on State Street, circa 1992. COURTESY MARY LANGENFELD

ABOVE: University of Wisconsin football team being given an opportunity for a goofy photo following their official team photo for the Hall of Fame Bowl in January 1995. COURTESY WISCONSIN STATE JOURNAL

ABOVE RIGHT: Madison Memorial Spartans hockey team celebrating their first goal of the night against Milwaukee University School, March 1998. COURTESY WISCONSIN STATE JOURNAL

RIGHT: Josie's Restaurant, 906 Regent Street, 1995. The eatery was owned by the Schuepbach-Jensen family between 1964 and 2007 before being lost to a fire. COURTESY JOANNE SCHUEPBACH JENSEN

OPPOSITE: Demonstrators clashing with police at the Great Midwest Marijuana Harvest Festival in September 1992. COURTESY WISCONSIN STATE JOURNAL

CHAPTER EIGHT
A NEW MILLENNIUM

Just after the dawn of the new century, the landscape and contours of downtown Madison changed forever with the launch of the Overture Center for the Arts, which replaced the Madison Civic Center.

Overture opened its doors on September 19, 2004, and thus began a new page in the history of Madison's arts and entertainment community. A donation of $205 million from Jerome Frautschi and his wife Pleasant Rowland created the sweeping, multi-venue Overture Center.

Less than a year later, the city lost a favorite landmark when St. Raphael Cathedral on West Main Street was destroyed by fire on March 14, 2005.

The nearly two decades in the 2000s have been hugely successful for UW athletics, fueled in large part by Barry and Bo – Alvarez and Ryan, that is.

Alvarez is credited with turning around the UW football

program during his tenure from 1990-2005, with one-game stints in 2012 and 2014 for bowl games. He finished his UW career with a record of 119-747-4, including 9-4 in bowl games.

Ryan and the UW men's basketball team became a national story with back-to-back Final Four appearances in 2014 and 2015. Ryan, who started as head coach at UW in 2001, has a record of 357-125 with the Badgers.

Madison has always been a political town, and never more so than in the spring 2011, when Gov. Scott Walker's controversial Act 10 legislation removed almost all power from public sector unions. The move caused a monthlong storm of protests from state workers, teachers and many others who opposed the Republican-led changes.

Four years later, the politics in Madison remain divided. And the Capitol remains the place where politics, policy and protesters often meet.

OPPOSITE: University of Wisconsin graduation, May 17, 2014. COURTESY KATHY SCHLIMGEN

ABOVE: University of Wisconsin wide receiver Lee Evans celebrating with the UW student section following a Wisconsin victory over the Akron Zips in which he made a critical 99-yard touchdown catch late in the game, September 6, 2003. Evans went on to be the 13th overall pick of the Buffalo Bills in the 2004 NFL draft. COURTESY WISCONSIN STATE JOURNAL

ABOVE: Kindergartner Susan Maloney (right) sharing her Halloween candy with second-grader Christopher Walsh as they walk home from school, October 29, 2003. COURTESY WISCONSIN STATE JOURNAL

ABOVE LEFT: Double rainbow looking east toward Downtown Madison from a hill near Mineral Point Road and Highway M, May 30, 2003. COURTESY WISCONSIN STATE JOURNAL

LEFT: Stevens Point Area Senior High softball team members watching an extra-innings game from their Uecker seats behind the outfield wall as they wait for their game to start during the WIAA State Softball Tournament quarterfinals at Goodman Diamond, June 10, 2003. COURTESY WISCONSIN STATE JOURNAL

ABOVE: Overview of Downtown Madison, including the Monona Terrace Convention Center in the foreground, 2005. COURTESY WISCONSIN STATE JOURNAL

OPPOSITE TOP LEFT: Theresa Gambino Pfeiffer's 50th anniversary at Josie's Restaurant, 906 Regent Street, circa 2002. From left: Donna Dirienzo Skoug, Pfeiffer, Alice Schmitz, Mary Ann Sveum, co-owner Joanne Schuepbach Jensen. COURTESY JOANNE SCHUEPBACH JENSEN

OPPOSITE BOTTOM LEFT: Joanne Schuepbach Jensen and Donna Dirienzo Skoug with the handmade Italian cookies (cuccidati) at Josie's Restaurant, 906 Regent Street, 2004.
COURTESY JOANNE SCHUEPBACH JENSEN

OPPOSITE RIGHT: Downtown Madison looking west along State Street, 2005. COURTESY WISCONSIN STATE JOURNAL

ABOVE: University of Wisconsin wide receiver Jonathan Orr reaching for a ball that was ruled incomplete after replay in a victory over the Purdue Boilermakers, October 22, 2005.
COURTESY WISCONSIN STATE JOURNAL

ABOVE LEFT: Athletic Director Pat Richter and former Chancellor Donna Shalala congratulating Coach Barry Alvarez following his final home game at Camp Randall Stadium as the University of Wisconsin's football coach, November 12, 2005. Alvarez led UW football to a record of 118–73–4 between 1990 and 2005.
COURTESY WISCONSIN STATE JOURNAL

LEFT: Wisconsin's Jack Skille scoring the winning goal on Cornell's David McKee in the third overtime period. The Badgers played Cornell in the NCAA 2006 Midwest Regional at the Resch Center in Green Bay on March 26, 2006. The Badgers won 1-0 in the third overtime.
COURTESY WISCONSIN STATE JOURNAL

OPPOSITE: Firefighters battling flames at St. Raphael Cathedral, 222 West Main Street, March 14, 2005. The landmark 150-year-old building was destroyed.
COURTESY WISCONSIN STATE JOURNAL

ABOVE: University of Wisconsin student Cathy Misher teaching a jazz, tap and ballet class to 2nd- and 3rd-graders at Madison School & Community Recreation's main building, March 12, 2007. COURTESY WISCONSIN STATE JOURNAL

RIGHT: Madison Museum of Contemporary Art in the 200 block of State Street shortly before opening, April 14, 2006. COURTESY WISCONSIN STATE JOURNAL

OPPOSITE TOP LEFT: Beatrice Levy, 6, of San Francisco embracing a cow at the Madison Farmer's Market Cow Parade, August 8, 2006. COURTESY WISCONSIN STATE JOURNAL

OPPOSITE BOTTOM LEFT: One of the five traveling groups of the Budweiser Clydesdales arriving at the Alliant Energy Center for the Midwest Horse Fair, April 16, 2007. COURTESY WISCONSIN STATE JOURNAL

OPPOSITE TOP RIGHT: Front columns of Memorial Union looking toward Library Mall, University of Wisconsin campus, October 30, 2006. The UW borrowed the idea of a collegiate social center from Cambridge and Oxford universities, and the Memorial Union, a 1926 Italian Renaissance-style building, was one of the first student unions in the United States. The Art Deco-inspired theater addition was built in 1938 with WPA funds. COURTESY WISCONSIN STATE JOURNAL

OPPOSITE BOTTOM RIGHT: Max Michalski and Leif Bergquist in one of 383 boats participating in the 29th annual Paddle & Portage, July 19, 2008. The event began in James Madison Park and finished in Olin Park. COURTESY WISCONSIN STATE JOURNAL

ABOVE: A sailboat passing in front of the setting sun on Lake Mendota, June 14, 2009. COURTESY WISCONSIN STATE JOURNAL

ABOVE LEFT: President Barack Obama speaking at a Madison rally, September 28, 2010. COURTESY WISCONSIN STATE JOURNAL

LEFT: University of Wisconsin quarterback Russell Wilson speaking during media day at Camp Randall Stadium, August 7, 2011. "I just want to be part of something special," the senior quarterback said that day. Wilson led the Badgers to a Big Ten title. COURTESY WISCONSIN STATE JOURNAL

OPPOSITE: The first lap of the 2.4-mile swim in Lake Monona for the 2008 Ford Ironman Wisconsin race, September 7, 2008. Following the swim, racers moved on to a 112-mile bike ride throughout Dane County and ended with a 26.2-mile run through Downtown Madison. COURTESY WISCONSIN STATE JOURNAL

ABOVE: Honor Flight Homecoming for WWII Navy Veteran Frederick "Fritz" Schlimgen, October 12th, 2012.
COURTESY KATHY SCHLIMGEN

RIGHT: The dome of Wisconsin's state Capitol building illuminated green and gold in anticipation of the Green Bay Packers appearance in Super Bowl XLV, February 2011.
COURTESY WISCONSIN STATE JOURNAL

OPPOSITE: Opponents of Wisconsin Gov. Scott Walker's budget repair bill amassing at the Capitol, March 2011.
COURTESY WISCONSIN STATE JOURNAL

BELOW: Nick Krantz and Rena Sletten, members of the Stoughton High School Norwegian Dancers, taking part in a traditional dance on the steps of the State Capitol, May 14, 2013. Celebrating the group's 60th year, the troupe honored the city's strong Norwegian heritage through a program of movement and music performed by 23 of the school's sophomores, juniors and seniors.
COURTESY WISCONSIN STATE JOURNAL

ABOVE: Dancers from the Kehl School of Dance performing on the Capitol steps at the Art Fair on the Square, July 2014.
COURTESY JEANNE KEELER

ABOVE RIGHT: Firefighters battling a warehouse fire in sub-zero temperatures at Windsor Building Systems, 314 Atlas Avenue, January 28, 2014.
COURTESY WISCONSIN STATE JOURNAL

RIGHT: Flames engulfing an apartment building under construction at the intersection of Lisa Ann Drive and Apollo Way, August 8, 2014. Fire and smoke could be seen Downtown across Lake Monona. The structure was leveled but no one was injured. COURTESY WISCONSIN STATE JOURNAL

LEFT: From left, University of Wisconsin forward Frank Kaminsky, guard Josh Gasser and forward Nigel Hayes embracing following a loss to Duke University in the NCAA men's basketball championship game at Lucas Oil Stadium in Indianapolis, April 6, 2015.
COURTESY WISCONSIN STATE JOURNAL

Wisconsin State Journal, Madison grew up together

The Wisconsin State Journal began as a weekly called The Madison Express in 1839. In 1848, the year Wisconsin became a state, David Atwood and Royal Buck bought the Express. Four years later, that newspaper was merged with several other papers and renamed the Wisconsin State Journal.

Atwood guided the newspaper for more than 40 years as its editor and publisher and, following his death, ownership changed several times. During the late 1800s and until 1906, the newspaper was led by Amos Wilder, father of playwright Thornton Wilder.

In 1911, veteran Washington and New York journalist Richard Lloyd Jones bought the paper and brought "big-city journalism" to Madison. Jones was a muckraker aligned with Progressive politicians, and by 1916, the State Journal was selling twice as many papers as its rival.

Jones then sold the State Journal to what is today Lee Enterprises Inc., which was then a small syndicate of papers founded in Ottumwa, Iowa.

The State Journal offices in the horse-and-buggy days of the 1890s were just off the Capitol Square on the first block of East Washington Avenue. STATE JOURNAL ARCHIVES

Richard Lloyd Jones became the State Journal's editor and publisher in 1911. WISCONSIN HISTORICAL SOCIETY IMAGE 3879

Outside the Wisconsin State Journal office on East Washington Avenue, circa 1881. David Atwood, second from left with white beard, and a partner launched the paper after buying the former Madison Express. STATE JOURNAL ARCHIVES

The building on South Carroll Street, shown in the late 1950s, that housed the Wisconsin State Journal, The Capital Times and Madison Newspapers Inc. STATE JOURNAL ARCHIVES

Reporters working in the Wisconsin State Journal newsroom on Carroll Street around 1970. STATE JOURNAL ARCHIVES

Exterior of the Madison Newspapers Inc. building on Fish Hatchery Road in the early 1980s. STATE JOURNAL ARCHIVES

Consolidation effort led to Fish Hatchery site

In 1948, the State Journal and afternoon competitor The Capital Times agreed to consolidate their publishing in one plant to be owned and managed by a new corporation, Madison Newspapers Inc. The newspapers maintained separate editorial staffs and news competition under this arrangement.

The State Journal, an afternoon newspaper for 97 years, also agreed to become the morning newspaper and publish the Sunday paper.

In the fall of 1975, the two newspapers moved to the present Capital Newspapers facility at 1901 Fish Hatchery Road.

601 University Avenue · 1914-1929

437 West Gilman Street · 1929-1939

SMART MOTORS WITHSTANDS THE TEST OF TIME

Despite meager beginnings and many worldly events that put other small businesses out of commission, Orren David Smart's head for business along with his determination, resourcefulness and tenacity, gave his company all the drive it needed to continue on for more than 100 years. Smart preferred diversification from his career beginnings of working in an auto garage and at a steel company to his choice of degree in college – engineering - to the many car brands he liked to sell at his dealership – 28 in total over the last 107 years. His company thrives on new opportunities, which continue to be imperative to its ongoing success.

Smart Motors has endured five physical moves since its beginning in a Waukesha livery stable in 1908. A fire forced the business out of its first Madison location at 617 University Avenue, so Smart set up shop again at 601 University Avenue. In 1929, he moved his business again, this time to a building he had built on Gilman Street. Ten years later he moved his

dealership to 2608 University Avenue, where it stayed until 1966 when the city of Madison acquired the property through eminent domain.

By the time the business was moved to Odana Road, Smart had turned the business over to his son, Frank James Smart and son-in-law Paul Emmerich. Together, the two men led the business through two significant changes that would secure its place within the auto market far into the future.

The first major change was the move to Odana Road, which doubled the dealership's service capacity and tripled its parts capacity. The location was more than twice the size of the one on University Avenue.

The second was during that same year, F.J. Smart was considering adding a Japanese franchise to the dealership, either Datsun or Toyota. Back in those days, Toyota was not commonly recognized and it was certainly not yet known in America for its reliability.

2608 University Avenue • 1939-1966

5901 Odana Road • 1966-2007

1966 - Odana Road Grand Opening

"I am so glad he made the decision to go with Toyota," said J.R. Smart, current president and C.E.O. of Smart Motors. "In 1966, we sold two Toyotas. It was certainly a challenge for us."

Fortunately, for Smart Motors, the oil embargo of 1973 successfully increased demand for Toyota's fuel efficient vehicles. As a result, many people in America began to notice the automaker, which naturally drove sales up.

Smart Motors has responded to Toyota's American success by becoming Wisconsin's largest Toyota dealer, one of the top 10 Toyota dealerships in the Midwest and the #1 retailer of hybrid vehicles.

Even though F.J. Smart likely didn't predict this success with Toyota, his son, J.R., believes his father definitely knew what he was doing.

SMART MOTORS

SINCE 1908

5901 Odana Road • 2008

By the time 2004 rolled around, the business had grown exponentially. Parking lots were overcrowded and customers were struggling to get timely appointments.

"That's when we decided to sell our Volvo franchise," J.R. said. "It was bittersweet because we had been a Volvo dealer for 40 years."

That's also when plans were made to construct the current dealership on Odana Road, which officially opened on December 3, 2007. The 110,000 square-foot Toyota dealership is the largest in the Midwest.

"It was a challenge to stay open during construction," J.R. said. "There was a lot of demolition going on and we had to operate out of trailers for awhile." But it all paid off. The new dealership has must-see customer service features, such as a choice of 600 on-site vehicles, computer kiosks, indoor auto pickup area, child play areas, wi-fi internet access, a cozy fireplace and flat-screen television, reading area, aquarium and fresh cookies and a variety of healthy fruits and snacks on site.

The new facilities also include an eight-bay lube station, one that's twice the size of the previous one, and features a larger customer lounge, two complimentary customer car washes, office space and retail displays.

In 2008, at the century celebratory mark of the dealership, Allen Foster, current V.P. at Smart Motors reflected on the company's success. He credits the dealership's – and the family's – commitment to customer care.

"Smart Motors was all about customer service before people were talking about customer service," Foster said.

"I remain dedicated to my family's business philosophy of; Commitment to Quality, Customer Satisfaction and Continuous Improvement," said J.R. "We have endured and thrived over the past 107 years due to our intense focus on meeting and exceeding the needs of our guests and teammates alike."

In that spirit, in May of 2010, Smart Motors bought Ball Body Shop. By owning this body shop, the company is able to operate a full-service body shop with capabilities to work on any vehicle on the road today.

Smart Motors opened NOVUS Glass Madison in 2011. This division of Smart Motors is a full service glass and windshield installation and repair operation. It is completely mobile and travels throughout southern Wisconsin.

NOVUS Glass Madison • 2011

Ball Body Shop - 2225 Eagle Drive, Middleton • 2013

By the time September of 2013 came, Ball Body Shop had undergone major external and internal renovations to expand capacity as well as customer amenities.

In September of 2014, the new vehicle prep department moved to a newly-constructed facility on Tokay Boulevard, The new facility has 18 service lifts installed as well as an auto butler for vehicle polishing and plenty of space for the company's maintenance staff.

Over the years, J.R. Smart continues to be proud of his family's history, dedication and progressiveness. He's also very proud of his employees at Smart Motors who continue to give their best to the customers.

"Just as my parents were proud of my brother and I for joining them in the family business," J.R. said, "I must admit that I am proud as a peacock that my daughter, Hannah, has made the decision to join me. Having just completed her degree from the UW, her addition will ensure the continuation of our proud heritage well into the future."

"I really have to credit my staff for our company's success," he said. "I couldn't do this without them. They are customer-focused and treat all customers as if they are guests in our staff's own homes."

The Wisconsin Historical Society's Archives has approximately 3 million images from more than 6,000 collections. Materials include photographs, negatives, films, architectural drawings, cartoons, lithographs, posters, and ephemeral materials from private, business, and governmental sources.

These visual materials document the rich social, economic, and political history of Wisconsin and the upper Midwest from the mid-1800s to the present, as well as those ethnic groups who helped shape its history. Image holdings are particularly strong in daily life from the turn of the century to the 1970s.

WISCONSIN HISTORICAL SOCIETY

The Historical Society supports a robust digitization program, and new digital content is added to wisconsinhistory.org every day, with over 8,000 images added per year.

These include the full range of materials available in our physical collections, and illustrate broad subject areas such as agriculture, domestic life, transportation, recreation, work, places and people.

There are approximately 20,000 digitized images of Madison, with the majority available to be reprinted or used for publication.

Discover the Society's historical images at wisconsinhistory.org/whi

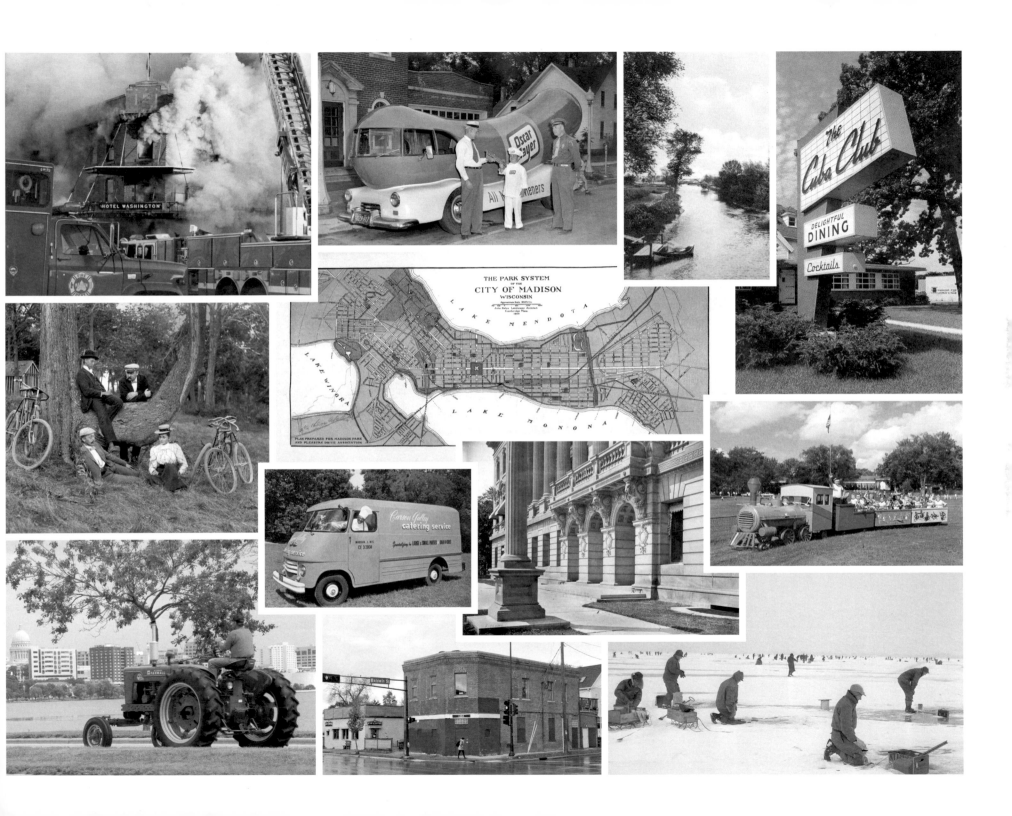

INDEX